Menagerie at the Manger

Menagerie at the Manger

Linda Allen

Illustrations by Scott Allen

The Editorial Annex

Oklahoma City/Edmond, Oklahoma

The Editorial Annex
Oklahoma City/Edmond, Oklahoma

Printed in China

ISBN 0-9725012-2-3

ACKNOWLEDGMENT

Menagerie at the Manger is a gift from God, and for that, I am thankful.

When I read the completed manuscript, I realized that I didn't know where all the ideas and words for this book came from. I still don't.

I just know they are a special gift, like the people who came along at just the right time with just the right help and encouragement to make my dream happen.

My special thanks to these angels: Stillwater Writers Mary Ellen Cooper, Audrey Eggers, Dennis Grondquist, Rachelle (Rey) Hanan, Simone, and Richard Ortez for reading the first draft; my minister, the Reverend Stan Warfield, First United Methodist

Church, Stillwater, Oklahoma, for reviewing the manuscript for theological accuracy; Todd, my son, for his life lessons in love and care of animals; Amy, my daughter-in-law, for grammar checking; Stephanie, my daughter-in-law, for encouraging Scott to meet the illustration deadlines of this book in the midst of planning and designing their wedding.

Also, the Star Sisters—creative and energetic Muses and friends; Mike Lorenz, Jeanne Devlin, and my husband, Don, for reviewing the final draft; Ron Long, for his ranching expertise and his answers to my questions about stables, mangers, and cattle; and deep gratitude to Richard M. Crum, my editor and publisher, for turning my idea and words into a finished book.

I especially thank my family and friends for their support, encouragement, praise, and patience as I chase my dream.

Dedicated to
all God's creatures

Contents

INTRODUCTION

Menagerie at the Manger

Thus ev'ry beast, by some good spell,
In the stable dark was glad to tell
Of the gift he gave Emmanuel.

— from "The Friendly Beasts"

A MEDIEVAL FRENCH CAROL

What could it have been like on the Nativity night over 2,000 years ago, a night of mystery and wonder that still astounds us today? A birth in a stable was not uncommon—except on this mysterious night; not a stable animal, but a special human was born there.

Stories and legends recount the wonder of the Nativity night. Much of what we know is based on common practices and customs of the time, but much of the Nativity story is left to speculation. No media recorded the miracle birth. Mary and Joseph left no journals or letters to describe their thoughts or emotions. The first visitors were the shepherds and the Magi, the Bible tells us, but they arrived after the birth.

There were, secular tales relate, other witnesses to the birth of the Christ Child—the menagerie at the manger. The donkey, sheep, and ox gathered to adore the Christ Child. Legends tell of other animals—a cat, a rooster, several birds—each quietly watching and worshiping in its own way.

Most of the menagerie were humble animals accustomed to hard work. Despite their lowly stature, they performed their tasks with a sense of nobility and dignity. At the Nativity, each gave its best gift, regardless of how simple it seemed.

In return, Mary and the Christ Child blessed the animals. They gave each one a distinctive marking or personality: the sheep, its soft wool; the donkey, the mark of the cross on its back; the robin, its red breast.

No animals are mentioned in the Bible's Nativity stories. But surely, common stable animals were honored guests at the birth of their Creator's son. Legends and folklore tell us this is so. These are their stories—the menagerie at the manger.

No Vacancy

And so it was, that while they were there,
the days were accomplished that
she should be delivered.
And she brought forth her first-born son,
and wrapped him in swaddling clothes, and
laid him in a manger; because there
was no room for them in the inn.

—Luke 2:6-7

More than 2,000 years ago, Caesar Augustus, the emperor of the Holy Roman Empire, ordered all citizens to participate in a census. This meant each person had to return to the city of his or her family's heritage. For many people, the order was an inconvenience and hardship. It was especially so for Joseph and Mary of Nazareth.

They were a young, newlywed couple, and Mary was nine months pregnant. In addition, they carried a secret unthinkable by any other human. They had been chosen to be the earthly parents of the Son of God.

Their journey to Bethlehem, the home of Joseph's family, covered more than 100 miles of desert and rugged hills. This bleak landscape could produce blinding sandstorms and venomous snakes and scorpions. These dangers were held back, however, to clear a path of safety for the Holy Family.

Weary after long days of travel, Joseph and Mary arrived in Bethlehem. They found the city crowded with other travelers who had come to register for the census. There were no vacancies in the inns or even in private homes. The only lodging offered was a cold stable. However crude it was, Joseph was probably lucky to find this shelter for Mary.

The Gospels give no specific setting or description for the Nativity. In Italian and Western European literature, the Nativity is usually a stable. Byzantine and earlier versions place it in a cave. Many references call the birthplace an inn.

This original holiday inn had no comforts modern-day travelers expect, no running water and no central heat. An opening in the roof admitted the only light. Straw on the floor was the only bed, and a manger remotely resembling a crib was the only piece of furniture.

The inn was shared by animals with their curious stares. Soon sheep would arrive in the company of shepherds, and camels would appear with the Magi. The stable was more like a zoo than an inn.

A stable is typically an open-air, weathered wood or stone structure, sometimes with a thatched roof. Construction is simple and practical. It has stalls for farm animals, such as cattle and sheep. Troughlike boxes, called mangers, hold hay and food for the animals.

When Joseph could find no other lodging, this uninviting shelter became the nursery for the Son of God. The manger became an improvised crib. It was filled with straw to make a soft cushion for the infant. The straw burst into fragrant, golden flowers, known as Our Lady's Bedstraw, according to legend. Stars fell from the heavens to become golden buttercups surrounding the manger and Christ Child. The dark, makeshift nursery suddenly turned into a glorious celebration of nature.

Huddled around the manger were a donkey, sheep, and perhaps a cat and an ox. Doves perched in the rafters, and chickens pecked at the dirt floor. Warm breaths, soft moos, loving coos, and excited clucking of God's creatures welcomed the wondrous baby into the world. The animals' gentle love helped warm the stable.

Many peoples have adapted the traditional setting and animals of the Nativity to fit their particular culture. Native American Nativity scenes are often set in a tepee with a buffalo and coyote looking on.

The exact birthplace of the Christ Child is unknown. We do know, however, He was born in simple surroundings with lowly animals at His crib. It was a humble beginning for a life that would forever change history and the world.

The Animals' Friend

Blessed are you, Lord God,
maker of all living creatures.
You called forth fish in the sea, birds
in the air, and animals on the land.
You inspired St. Francis to call all of
them his brothers and sisters....

— from *The Blessing of Pets*

A TRADITIONAL PRAYER OF THE FEAST OF SAINT FRANCIS

Saint Francis of Assisi, the animals' friend, is known as the patron saint of the animal kingdom. He is credited with creating the first live reenactment of the Nativity. In the 13th century, many people could not read. To communicate God's love to them, Saint Francis staged a reenactment of the Nativity in 1223. He used live animals, descendants of the animals that legend places at the manger. An ox, a donkey, and some sheep surrounded the hay-filled crib. This living Nativity made the drama of Christ's birth come alive for the people.

The life of Saint Francis is a reverse story of rags to riches. Giovanni (John) Francesco Bernardone was born into a wealthy family in Assisi, Italy, around 1180. He was a spirited and even rebellious youth.

The reversal of his fortune and carefree lifestyle was a deliberate choice. He gave up his family's wealth to live with the poor and to walk with the animals he considered his family. He chose to emulate the life of Christ and experience the love of God through poverty.

As a young man, John fought in a war with the neighboring town of Perugia in 1202. The conflict caused a powerful change in his life. He was captured and as a prisoner suffered a high fever. In a dream during his illness, he heard a voice begging him to come home. John returned, a changed person. He gave up his wealth and privileges to live with the poor.

A second turning point in John's life came as he prayed in the Chapel of St. Damian near Assisi. In his meditation, he heard another voice. "Go and repair my house," the voice commanded. He believed the instruction was from God and he obeyed. He began repairs on the chapel immediately. John became devoted to prayer and preaching. He also established the Order of Friars

Minor—known as Franciscans. They live in poverty as a way to share God's love. Just like Christ, Saint Francis chose 12 followers to assist him when he began his ministry.

Although his religious contributions are significant, Saint Francis is best known for his love and care of animals. He was an animal rights activist long before such issues became popular and political. He walked and talked with the animals and even preached to the birds. Saint Francis had a charismatic and intuitive communication with all of nature, including trees and plants, the stars, the moon, and the sun. He befriended all creations in nature and gave his beloved family members names like Brother Wolf and Sister Moon.

A man talking to animals and plants was a curiosity to people of that time. Many legends arose about Saint Francis' magical powers with animals. He was said to have rescued many animals and to have tamed wild beasts.

One story tells how he calmed a wolf that had been terrorizing a village, killing people and other animals. Saint Francis spoke gently to the animal and offered his hand in friendship. He promised the wolf it would be fed and protected by the village if it gave up its violent ways. The wolf nodded its head in agreement and extended its paw to Saint Francis.

From that time on, the wolf walked through the streets of the village, threatening no one and being fed and cared for by the people as a companion and a familiar sight in the village. When it died, it was greatly missed.

Saint Francis traveled barefoot so he wouldn't harm the grass and plants. He moved insects out of his path so he would not step on them. So great was his love for nature, he refused to use a staff or cane to avoid cutting down trees and plants. He expressed this love in "Canticle of the Creatures," a tribute to all living things.

Christmas was Saint Francis' favorite time of year. He lobbied the emperor of Rome to pass a law to give food to the animals on Christmas Day in celebration of their storied roles in the Nativity.

This tradition is still honored today as people leave choice food for the animals. Wheat sheaves are saved from the harvest in some countries for the birds. Cattle, sheep, and horses often receive an extra bale of hay as a Christmas gift from their owners.

Saint Francis died in 1226. He was canonized by the Vatican in 1228 and named the Patron Saint of Ecology in 1979. The Feast of Saint Francis is celebrated on October 4. This day is set aside for the blessing of the animals in honor of the compassionate saint.

The well-known Prayer of Saint Francis preserves his philosophy:

Lord, make me an instrument of your peace,
Where there is hatred, let me sow love;
where there is injury, pardon,
where there is doubt, faith,
where there is despair, hope,
where there is darkness, light,
where there is sadness, joy.
O Divine Master, grant that I may not so much seek
to be consoled as to console,
to be understood as to understand,
to be loved as to love.
For it is in giving that we receive,
it is in pardoning that we are pardoned,
and it is in dying that we are born to eternal life.

The Christ Bearer

"I," said the donkey, shaggy and brown,
"I carried His mother up hill and down;
I carried her safely to Bethlehem town."

—from "The Friendly Beasts"

A MEDIEVAL FRENCH CAROL

Probably the most recognized animal of the Nativity is the donkey. It served from the birth of Christ to His death as His transportation and appointed companion.

At first thought, it may seem strange that the donkey and Christ are associated. But in some ways they are similar. Both experienced ridicule and taunts; the donkey for its physical appearance, distinctive voice, and reputation for being stubborn; Christ for His unwavering claim to be the Son of God and His message of love, peace, and acceptance for everyone.

Ancient Greeks and Romans held another view of the donkey, however, and in no way did it resemble Christ. For the Greeks and Romans, the donkey represented drunkenness, laziness, lust, and promiscuity. It was associated with their gods, Bacchus and Dionysus.

Yet, even with such a reputation, the humble donkey was chosen to be the Christ Bearer. This title of honor was given to it by the early Christian church because it carried Mary to Bethlehem during her pregnancy. It also carried Mary and the Christ Child on their flight to Egypt. Its last service for Christ was on Palm Sunday. The donkey carried Him into Jerusalem before the Crucifixion.

In biblical times, donkeys were the transportation of choice for peasants, judges, and prophets. Even kings rode them on occasion. Christ fulfilled all these roles in His life—from carpenter's son to the King of Kings—so it was fitting for him to ride a donkey.

One legend about the donkey's appearance and distinctive voice comes from a story told by Saint Francis. One day, he heard the sad braying of a small donkey. Saint Francis asked about its sadness. From the beginning of time, the donkey had been a beast of burden, carrying heavy loads on its small back. People and other animals always made fun of how it sounded. Their ridicule didn't seem fair to the donkey.

Saint Francis explained that of all the animals God had created, the donkey was His favorite. God liked the donkey because it was very spirited and lively, and it enjoyed all of life's pleasures. It was always romping and kicking up its heels and singing beautiful songs of praise to its Creator.

One day, the donkey saw its reflection in a pond and realized it was truly the most handsome of all the animals. Instead of its usual frolicking, the donkey began to strut and make fun of how other animals looked—the camel with its hump, the giraffe with its long neck, the zebra with its stripes, the monkey with its long tail.

Finally, the animals had had enough of the donkey's

name-calling and insults. They decided to take matters into their own hands. The monkeys grabbed the donkey's short ears and began to pull.

The donkey was in so much pain, the only sound it could make was "hee-haw, hee-haw." The more it cried, the harder the monkeys pulled. They tugged and stretched the donkey's ears until they drooped almost to its shoulders. Then a chimpanzee grabbed the donkey's tail and began to pull in the opposite direction.

The poor donkey's loud cries created such a commotion that God had to intervene. He reprimanded both the donkey and the monkeys. God scolded the donkey for taking advantage of His favor and for ridiculing and laughing at the other creatures.

As punishment, the donkey's laughter would become the off-key *hee-haw* sound that distinguishes it from all other animals. The donkey's ears would remain long and droopy, and its tail would be scrawny and scraggly like a rope. The donkey would forever be a beast of burden, destined to carry the heaviest loads.

A more sympathetic version tells how the donkey came to have such long, droopy ears. While carrying Mary and the Christ Child through the Holy Land, it tried to cross a river and became stuck in quicksand.

Fortunately, Saint Gabriel was looking down from heaven and saw the donkey's predicament. He reached down and grabbed the sinking donkey by its ears. The harder Saint Gabriel pulled, the longer the donkey's ears grew. After much pulling, Saint Gabriel rescued the donkey from danger, but not before the donkey's ears had been stretched out long and limp.

The donkey's grating hee-haw voice may be explained by yet another legend. For many years, Joseph and Mary and the Christ Child hid from King

Herod in Egypt. When Joseph decided to move his family back to Nazareth, the same donkey again carried Mary and the Christ Child.

One night while camped along the side of the road, the donkey heard horses approaching. Fearing Herod's soldiers were coming to kill the Holy Family, the donkey neighed and whinnied as loud as it could. Its voice sounded like a familiar horse's voice. Joseph, Mary, and the Christ Child slept soundly through all the donkey's commotion to waken them.

As the soldiers drew nearer, the donkey began to panic, and it prayed for a louder voice. When it neighed again, its voice was the loud bray donkeys have had ever since. Its harsh "hee-haw" startled the sleeping family awake and gave them enough time to hide from Herod's soldiers.

The donkey is a stubborn, but gentle-spirited and

intelligent animal. For centuries, donkeys have carried almost everything, from common stones and lumber to exotic spices and gems. Donkeys are even more popular than horses as pack animals. Their small, round, flexible hooves make them surefooted across rough terrain. They can travel long distances. Their steady gait can cover about 15 miles per hour.

The donkey was the perfect transportation for Mary on her trip to Bethlehem. The donkey must have sensed how precious its cargo was. It trudged on, step after step, without balking or halting. Its steady pace made the long, tedious, and dangerous trip as comfortable as possible for the mother-to-be.

Mary rewarded the kind donkey for its gentle journey. She gave it a special marking, a cross of dark hair on its back. This cross played two roles in events to come more than 30 years later.

First, it allowed Christ to recognize the colt of Mary's donkey. This colt became the Christ Bearer into Jerusalem on Palm Sunday. Christ chose to ride a donkey because it is a symbol of peace, while the horse is a symbol of war.

Second, the cross of hair on the donkey's back foreshadowed the Cross of the Crucifixion awaiting Christ at the end of His Jerusalem journey.

In legend and life, the lowly donkey supported Christ from the joy of His birth to the sorrow of His death. It earned the title of Christ Bearer with quiet dignity, devotion, and courage.

Mary Had a Little Lamb

"I," said the sheep with the curly horn,
"I gave Him my wool for a blanket warm;
He wore my coat on Christmas morn."

—from "The Friendly Beasts"

A MEDIEVAL FRENCH CAROL

"Mary had a little lamb, its fleece was white as snow..."—a simple child's rhyme or a deeper theological statement?

In 1830, Sarah Joseph Hale wrote the popular child's verse "Mary Had a Little Lamb." It is supposedly based on a true incident. Although it may not have been the intent of Ms. Hale, the opening stanzas of the verse convey spiritual and religious significance.

It is possible, and even probable, that Mary—the mother of Christ—did have a little lamb. In biblical times, it was a common custom for a young girl to keep a female lamb as a pet. Her lamb was never used for food or sacrifice.

The lamb represents innocence, gentleness, and purity. It is the only animal that Satan cannot destroy or possess, according to legends. Perhaps certain lambs were used as sacrificial offerings to counter Satan's evil. Their wool, or fleece, is usually white, a symbolic color of purity. Black was an unacceptable color for sacrifices. Even today, the term *black sheep* has a negative meaning—a social or family outcast.

There are hundreds of references to sheep and shepherds in the Bible; some are parables, some are metaphors. Christ is frequently referred to as the Lamb of God, or *Agnus Dei* in Latin. His cousin, John the Baptist, gave Him this name. *Agnus Dei* is a resurrection symbol of a lamb carrying a banner or flag. Crucifixes in the early church carried the image of a lamb, a symbol of sacrifice, instead of the figure of the crucified Christ.

Christ is portrayed as the Good Shepherd. He protects His followers like a shepherd watches over his flock. Christ's followers are people who need guidance, much like sheep.

Judaic law governed many life practices and rituals in biblical times. The law determined which animals were clean and appropriate for religious sacrifices. Sheep were considered clean. Only perfect lambs could be presented for sacrificial offerings. This required the shepherd to keep the flock not only safe but also in perfect health.

Sheep have been a mainstay in people's lives for centuries. They provide two basic human needs—food, and wool to make clothing and blankets for warmth. Sheep herding is a centuries-old lifestyle and occupation still practiced in many countries today.

Shepherds lead a solitary life dedicated to the sheep. They spend long, lonely hours watching and guarding the flock. Shepherds need quick wits and strong, agile muscles to protect the sheep from predators. They also have to feed the sheep, provide shelter for them, and lead them to and from the pastures each day. Furthermore, shepherds must be auditors—counting sheep, not to cure insomnia, but to provide a correct accounting of all the animals.

Sheep are docile and defenseless animals. They have no fangs or claws for protection. This makes them easy targets for predators, such as wolves, hyenas, wildcats, and coyotes.

Sheep and wolves are frequently paired in the Bible, folktales, and nursery rhymes to illustrate good and evil. The innocence of sheep is in sharp contrast to the guile of the wolf. The Bible advises to beware of false prophets dressed in sheepskins. Little Red Riding Hood's story is a similar lesson for children about trust and truth. The Bible predicts a time when the conflict will end, and the lamb and the wolf shall lie down together in peace.

The shepherds tending their sheep under the Bethlehem night sky were terrified when an angel of God appeared before them. Their fears were calmed when the angel told them good news of great joy: "A Saviour has been born to you. He is Christ the Lord."

The shepherds wanted to hurry to Bethlehem to celebrate the Christ Child's birth. But no good shepherd would ever leave sheep untended. To do so would expose the flock to danger from predators. Either the sheep would have to travel with the shepherds or one shepherd would have to stay behind and guard the flock.

How it was decided who would go and who would stay is unclear. But some sheep traveled with the shepherds, according to legend. What a gift their presence was. They formed a woolly wall of warmth to block the cold night air from the Newborn. Some sheep gave their thick fleece to provide a blanket for the baby.

Were the sheep sheared or did they shed their wool some other way? Legend doesn't say.

As a gift of thanks, the Christ Child blessed them with soft wool instead of the coarse and stringy strands they originally wore.

Shepherds and sheep at the manger worshiping the Christ Child on the Nativity night—how could they know they would become symbolic of Christ from His birth to His death?

Ruminating Ruminants

"I," said the cow, all white and red,
"I gave Him my manger for his bed;
I gave Him my hay to pillow his head."

—from "The Friendly Beasts"

A MEDIEVAL FRENCH CAROL

What were they thinking about on the Nativity night—the ruminating ruminants? Centuries later, there is no way we can know what the animals knew that night, except through legend.

Cattle, oxen, and camels are cud-chewing animals. These animals often have a mouthful of cud (previously digested food) that they slowly rechew. Near the manger they stood, slowing chewing their cud as if pondering a great thought.

What a miraculous vision must have been running through their heads. There, before their very eyes, the Son of God was born.

Different Nativity scenes show a variety of animals from the bovine family—the cow, bull, ox. Any of these animals could have been in the stable at the Nativity. Native American Nativities often include a buffalo instead of a cow or ox.

Could one of the animals have been the auroch, or *Bos primigenius*? The auroch was used to plow fields, move heavy objects, and transport people, supplies, and building materials in the time of Christ. It was also a source of meat, milk, and leather for people.

The auroch lived in Europe, Asia, and North Africa, but has been extinct for 1,300 years. Sketches of aurochs have been found in caves in France; the images reflect the art graffiti of early man.

Most likely, the bovines at the stable were the cow and ox. They are strongly associated with agricultural uses. To provide enough food to live on in ancient times required a minimum of one ox to work the land. Anyone who owned a herd of oxen possessed great wealth and high social status.

In many cultures today, both the cow and bull are sacred celestial animals. Their crescent-shaped horns reflect the moon in its waxing and waning phases. Lunar gods and goddesses wear horns on their heads to symbolize the moon. Another popular lunar connection is the child's nursery rhyme with the "cow jumping over the moon." The frothy milk from sacred celestial cows became the Milky Way and nourished the earth with rain, claim ancient legends.

The bull is honored in Greek mythology. Zeus, the supreme god of the Greeks, hurled the bull, Taurus, into the skies. It landed between the constellations Aries and Orion and became the constellation Taurus. Taurus appears to be grazing peacefully while protecting the cows and calves of his herd in the night skies.

Another Greek myth uses a bull as the protagonist in the love story of Zeus and Europa. Europa was the daughter of King Agenor of Tyre. To attract her attention, Zeus disguised himself as a strong, sleek, white bull with mother-of-pearl horns and a silver moon symbol on his forelock. One day, Europa noticed this magnificent animal, different from the others in her father's black herd. Her curiosity tempted her to approach the handsome animal. When she did, the bull kneeled so she could climb upon its back.

Europa expected only a gentle ride around the pasture. The bull whisked her away to Crete, instead. There, Zeus transformed himself from a bull back into a god and made Europa his queen. As a special gift for her, he presented her all the land she could see from her new island home. This land was named in her honor, the continent we now know as Europe.

The term *Holy Cow*, is more than just an expression of astonishment. Throughout history, cows and bulls have served a variety of purposes in world religions, from idols and sacred symbols to sacrifices.

References to cows and calves appear throughout the Bible. A fattened calf was served on festive occasions. Calves were often sacrificed as a sign of repentance in the Old Testament. A golden calf was created as an idol to worship by Israelites waiting impatiently for Moses to return from Mount Sinai.

In the Hindu religion, the cow is a sacred animal that should not be injured or mistreated. Bulls were holy to the ancient Egyptians and were praised in Greek and Roman mythology.

Islamic, Buddhist, and Turkish traditions claim celestial bulls carry the world upon their horns and backs. If the bulls should stumble or become enraged or wild, the world is jostled and juggled about on their horns. This motion creates violent earthquakes and severe weather, so said wise men trying to explain unexplainable events in the ancient world.

The cow or ox played a significant role at Christ's birth. The animal stood close to the Newborn's manger-cradle, slowly chewing its cud, perhaps mixed with a little hay. Such animals are often labeled clumsy because of their size and brawn. The clichés *clumsy as an ox* and *bull in the china shop* describe their awkwardness in a confined space.

But on the Nativity night, in an enclosed stable, there were no bellows, snorts, or kicking. The animals' breaths were soft and muffled. Gently, they knelt in honor of the Christ Child, and still do at midnight on Christmas Eve, according to some legends.

The cow gave up its manger of hay to serve as a cradle for the infant. The cow and sheep stood together close to the Christ Child, Mary, and Joseph and created a protective barrier from the night's chill wind. Their soft breaths surrounded the Holy Family with a cloud of love and warmth. Gentle moos blended with dove coos to create a lullaby, the first Christmas carol.

Ringing in Christmas with joyous bells began with a cowbell. When the shepherds arrived in Bethlehem, their questions about where to find the birthplace of the special baby created great excitement. Crowds gathered as curious people flocked to see for themselves.

Sitting by himself along the roadside was a small, blind boy. He overheard the excited talk about the baby, and he wanted to visit the stable with everyone else. But, the crowd was in such haste, no one heard his pleas to be led to the stable.

The crowd rushed past and left the boy by himself. Suddenly, from somewhere in the distance, came the jingle of a cow's bell. "Maybe," he thought, "that cow is in the same stable as the baby." The boy listened closely to the bell.

Slowly, he got up and carefully followed the jingling sound. It grew louder and louder as he came closer and closer. Soon he was standing at the manger worshiping the Christ Child. From that night to this, the legend resounds loud and clear: Let the bells ring out with joy during the Christmas season—church bells, sleigh bells, and even cow bells.

The Cat in the Cradle

He will kill mice, and he will be kind to babies when he is in the house, just as long as they do not pull his tail too hard.

The Cat that Walked by Himself—Rudyard Kipling

Every good stable or barn usually has a cat, the resident mouser, to keep the rodent population controlled. Because it performs a valuable service, the cat is respected in the community of stable animals.

Although a cat does not often appear in many Nativity scenes, it is easy to believe that a cat was close by the crib that Holy Night. Early paintings of the Holy Family show a cat in the background. Leonardo da Vinci drew several sketches of the Madonna and Child with a playful kitten.

Cats have experienced a love-hate relationship with people throughout history. They have lived in close association with humans for at least 5,000 years. Probably the first tame cats were in North Africa. They became domesticated from their wild ancestor, *Felix silvestris*. Popular cartoon names like Felix and Sylvester come from this reference.

In ancient Egypt and Rome, cats enjoyed near god-like status. Cats guarded tombs and pyramids in Egypt. They were so honored that the penalty for killing one, even by accident, was death.

With the advent of Christianity, all things associated with pagan religions, including plants and animals, were banned from church practices and rituals. Christians viewed the cat as a pagan idol. It represented all forms of evil, including the sins of laziness, backbiting, promiscuity, gossip, and deceit.

For Medieval people, cats represented the devil, witches, vampires, and black magic. They were publicly tortured and killed to rid society of its evil deeds. Cats were even thrown from towers. Because many survived the fall and walked away seemingly unhurt, special powers were attributed to them, including the survival rate of nine lives.

Farmers would bury a cat in a field as a warning of death for anything evil that came along. In this way, farmers hoped to ensure a good harvest. Black cats were perhaps the most feared. They were an omen of bad luck. That superstition continues today.

Legends about the cat date to Noah and the ark. The cat was not created with the rest of the animals, Hebrew and Arabian legends claim. Instead, its first appearance was on the ark with Noah.

How long the ark would be adrift on the floodwaters Noah had no idea. He was afraid that the mice would eat all the food and supplies long before the ark reached safety. To put Noah at ease, God caused a sleeping lion to sneeze a great "Achoo!" The mighty sneeze created a miniature version of the lion to be the ark's resident mouser.

The ark was the setting for a second cat legend. It

had to do with the Manx cat. The Manx originally sported a lush, bushy tail. It wasn't the proverbial curiosity of the cat that caused it to wear just a stub or no tail at all. It was greed and willfulness.

It all happened when the many kinds of animals were boarding the ark two by two. The Manx cats playfully perched on the gangplank to watch the other animals board. When the rats and mice tried to come up, the cats pounced on them and ate as many as they could. Noah patiently pleaded for the cats to come aboard, but they ignored him.

At the last moment, the cats raced up the gangplank to get into the ark before Noah closed the doors. They made it inside—almost made it, that is. As Noah slammed the doors shut, their beautiful Manx tails were caught and cut off, left on the wrong side of the ark—forever.

Other legends describe the role of the cat at the Nativity. One tells of a pregnant cat in the stable. It gave birth to kittens at the same time as Christ's birth. This cat's revered name in Italian legends is *gatta della Madonna*. Mary blessed the cat with the marking of a cross on its back; the cross commemorates the shared births of the Christ Child and the kittens.

Another legend focuses on a tabby. Like any normal baby, the Christ Child would cry and fuss. After all, a manger was not the most comfortable baby crib. Once, when Mary was having trouble getting Him to sleep, she asked the stable animals to help calm Him. A tabby jumped up in response. It cuddled in the manger next to the baby. The cat's meow became a gentle purr, putting the Christ Child to sleep with a feline lullaby.

Even after the other animals had gone to sleep, the cat in the cradle continued its soothing purr throughout the night. The next morning Mary touched the cat's forehead, leaving the image of an "M" as a sign of her favor. The "M" reminds the world what a good mother the cat was. The touch of the Madonna can still be seen on many household cats today.

All cats were wild until the Nativity, another legend claims. Mary rewarded the cat in the cradle and all its feline cousins with the gift of tameness so they could be our beloved pets.

By the Dawn's Early Light

It faded on the crowing of the cock.
Some say that ever 'gainst that season comes
Wherein our Saviour's birth is celebrated,
the bird of dawning singeth all night long....
So hallow'd and so gracious is the time.

Hamlet, act 1, scene 1—Shakespeare

The chicken family is a busy group of birds, scratching and pecking at the ground for food and scurrying in all directions. Chickens seem to be in constant motion. Stables and barns are favorite nesting places for them because the hay provides a warm, safe shelter for their young. In like fashion, the stable on the Nativity night provided a warm, safe shelter for Mary, Joseph, and their Newborn.

Characterization of animals varies from culture to culture. In the United States and some parts of Europe, the chicken is considered a foolish and even cowardly bird. Because of its small head and equally small brain, the chicken often seems stupid. It is the brunt of jokes, insults, and ridicule. The schoolyard taunt of *chicken* describes a lack of bravery and stands as a universal label of cowardice.

The chicken's personality is part of popular childhood stories. Chicken Little ran around the barnyard in a panic over his imaginary fear that the sky was falling. Such a story reinforces the belief that the chicken is foolish and easily excited and spooked.

The story of the Little Red Hen presents another side of a chicken's personality, however. She planted, tended, and harvested a crop of wheat all by herself. The Little Red Hen exhibits the characteristics of independence and determination.

Both descriptions are probably true in part. The hen is a protective mother. Her behavior gives us the phrase *mother hen* to describe a doting parent. The hen shoos and gathers her chicks under her outspread wings at any hint of danger. Like Chicken Little, the hen may anticipate dangers that don't exist.

The pride of the chicken family is the rooster. The rooster is a handsome bird with colorful tail feathers and a bright red comb and wattle. It struts its plumage with a take-charge personality around the barnyard. Its boastful posture gives us the *cock of the walk* description of some dandy who is quite pleased with his appearance or accomplishments.

There were probably hens in the stable on the night of Christ's birth. But, it was the rooster that announced the miracle birth to the world.

Perhaps the Star of Wonder shining over the stable was as bright as daybreak and awoke the rooster. Its joyous crowing roused the bees. Other birds, too, were startled by the rooster's midnight *cock-a-doodle-doo*.

In ancient times, birds were reliable and fast messengers. This Holy Night, they took flight, people say, to spread the news of Christ's birth.

Some cultures believe the rooster wakes the sun each day with its crowing instead of the sun waking the rooster. The Nativity is the only time in history when the rooster crowed at midnight, so legends claim. In Spain and Latin America, the traditional Christmas Eve mass at midnight is named *Misa del Gallo* (Mass of the Rooster).

The rooster also played a role in the events leading to the Crucifixion. Christ shared the news of His impending death with His disciples at the Last Supper. There, Peter learned he would deny Christ three times before the cock crowed. He steadfastly and vehemently swore he would not disown his friend. But, that's exactly what Peter did, not once, but three times just before the cock crowed.

So, believers claim, the rooster served as a messenger at the two most important events in Christ's life. It greeted His birth and warned of His death. Paradoxically, both events were good news for the world.

Nestled in the Christmas Tree

"I," said the dove from the rafters high,
"I cooed him to sleep so He would not cry;
We cooed Him to sleep, my mate and I."

—from "The Friendly Beasts"

A MEDIEVAL FRENCH CAROL

Probably the most recognized and popular birds of Christmas are the partridge in the pear tree, two turtledoves, three French hens, four calling birds, six geese a-laying, and seven swans a-swimming. They populate the much-sung "Twelve Days of Christmas."

For years, debates have argued the song's origin and its symbolism. Some arguments attach religious significance to the song, each day representing a theological meaning or symbol. Others state it is simply a child's nonsense song for entertainment. Whatever the reason, the song calls attention to the importance of birds in our Christmas traditions.

Birds of rainbow-colored feathers flocked together at the manger. From ospreys to ostriches, eagles to emus, and hummingbirds to herons, all celebrated the wonderful birth of the Christ Child. Legends, folklore, and even history describe their roles in the Nativity.

The dove is the universal symbol of peace and love. It made multiple appearances in the life of Christ. It first appeared in a dream to the parents of Mary before her birth. The dove symbolized the important role she would play in religious history. A second dove perched on Joseph's staff, a sign to him that Mary was to become his wife.

At the Nativity, the soft, cooing lullaby of the doves soothed the Christ Child to sleep. Joseph brought two white doves as an offering to the priests at the temple when the infant received the ritual blessings.

Later at Christ's baptism, the Spirit of God descended from the heavens like a dove. And, doves appeared at Christ's resurrection as symbols of the love and peace in His life.

The robin was also present at the Nativity, a legend claims. But it was not the familiar red-breasted songster that welcomes spring. It was an ordinary, nondescript, brown bird.

In the stable, there was a small fire, mostly embers. It had been left untended in the excitement of the birth. Although wrapped in swaddling clothes and cuddled on a bed of hay, the baby still shivered in the night air. The robin tried to waken the ox and donkey so they could breathe on the fire to rekindle the flames.

But they dozed, oblivious to the bird's fuss. So, the small, brown bird used its tiny wings as bellows. It flapped and flapped its wings and fanned the embers into a warming flame.

The bird got so close to the flame, however, that it singed its breast feathers. The scorched feathers slowly turned a ruddy hue. Mary blessed the brave robin with this gift, a red feather vest to wear over its heart forever as a symbol of its love and courage.

Like the donkey, dove, and rooster, the robin played a recurring role in the life of Christ. One robin lived near the gates of Jerusalem, legend claims. It feasted on morsels dropped by travelers and traders.

On Good Friday, the robin's curiosity was piqued by a strange commotion. A throng of soldiers and common people were shouting and throwing stones at three men carrying crosses. The puzzled robin followed the crowd to Calvary. The small bird was horrified at what the soldiers had done to the men.

Two of the men were each strapped to a cross. The third man was nailed to His cross. It was this man who caught the robin's attention. He had kind, weary eyes.

The robin flew to the man with the kind eyes and tried to pull the nails out of His bleeding hands. The little bird tugged and tugged, but even with all its might, its beak was not strong enough to loosen the nails. Not willing to give up, the little bird flew to the man's head and began pulling out the thorns piercing His forehead. Some soldiers tried to kill the robin with stones, but a centurion forbade anyone to harm the little bird.

The robin stayed with Christ until His death. Shortly before His last breath, Christ blessed the robin. The bird's breast feathers, stained with Christ's blood, would always remain red. This would be a sign, Christ promised, that people would forever remember the bird's compassion, courage, and love.

Another bird said to have been blessed that Holy Night was the stork. The stork is a very nurturing bird. It has the honor of delivering babies in folklore stories. In the Nativity stable, the stork noticed the Christ Child's bed was a nest of hay in the manger.

Although hay can be soft and fragrant, it certainly was not fitting bedding for a child destined to become the King of Kings. The stork wanted to give the child something to honor Him and to make Him comfortable. It plucked the downy feathers from its breast to cushion His head. To thank it for its gift of comfort and love, the Christ Child blessed the stork and made it the patron of babies everywhere.

The owl isn't usually associated with the Christmas season, and for good reason. The owl was the one bird that chose not to visit the Nativity, according to legends.

When the Magi began their journey to Bethlehem, they invited all the birds to accompany them. Fluttering, chirping, and chattering, the birds left their nests, eager to experience the big event. Only the skeptical owl refused to leave its comfy nest to fly to unknown parts on just a rumor. Still today, we hear its haunting "Who?" "Who?" questions about the wonderful baby.

Many countries have traditions and customs to

honor birds at Christmas. In Hungary, people save the last sheaf of harvest grains and give it to birds on New Year's morning. Corn is placed on rooftops in Germany on Christmas Eve. In Sweden, a sheaf of grain atop a tall pole on Christmas Day treats birds.

In ancient times, these customs may have been offerings to ancestral spirits. Through the years, they have taken their place as holiday traditions enjoyed by the entire family.

A popular U.S. tradition comes from these European customs. Trees are decorated with savory treats, such as garlands of berries and unsalted popcorn, for the birds. Birds also enjoy a smorgasbord of seeds and grains in their feeders or scattered on the ground for Christmas dinner. In return, people enjoy a Christmas Day of bird watching and bird caroling.

Finding a bird's nest tucked among the Christmas

tree branches is one of the luckiest Yuletide traditions. It predicts good fortune through the coming year. Some nests are store-bought, others are the real thing abandoned by a migrating species. Some people place three gold-colored eggs in the nest—a sign of health, wealth, and happiness.

The Eensy-Weensy Spider

The spider taketh hold with her hands,
and is in kings' palaces.

—Proverbs 30:28

Above the Nativity stable, the Star of Bethlehem shone in brilliant splendor. Its rays beamed through cracks in the stable walls. High in one corner, seen by no one, a spider wove its web as intricate as tatted lace. The delicate threads sparkled in the star's bright glow. The web covered a crack in the wall, blocking the cold night air from the Holy Family, or so legends say.

Spiders have a bad reputation. Just the sight of one strikes fear and panic into the hearts of many people. While some spiders are poisonous, many play a major role in controlling the world's insect population. Some spiders are a gardener's best friend. They rid the garden of pests. The weight of insects eaten by spiders is greater than the total weight of the entire human population, studies indicate. Without spiders, the world would be overrun by insects.

The web the spider spins is its home. It weaves its dwelling from silken threads produced by its body. This ability makes the spider a natural curiosity.

A spider web is a marvel of art, engineering, science, and geometry. The spider secretes a liquid protein from silk glands, called spinnerets. As the silk strands are released, they harden to form the warp and woof of the web. The web appears fragile and delicate, but it is stronger than it looks. Some spiders' silk is up to five times stronger than a steel thread of the same diameter.

To begin its fanciful web weaving, the spider attaches a silken thread to a plant leaf, a tree branch, or some other strong structure. The spider works from the outside points inward, often rappelling to create a geometric design of angles. It uses this elaborate net to entangle its prey. Once caught in a web, a hapless insect can't escape, and soon it is devoured by the spider.

The spider's web is the source of legends and symbols in many cultures. Ancient Egyptians and Greeks believed the spider was a symbol of the Fates that controlled a person's destiny. The Celts believed the web was like the maze of life. It presented difficulties and challenges that each person must face and overcome. For some Christians, the spider represents the devil, and the web, his trap of evil.

Native American dream catchers represent the spider's web. They are modeled after the web of Iktome, the Keeper of All Dreams. A traditional dream catcher is fashioned from a willow hoop. Sinew threads are woven in the center of the hoop to represent the threads of a spider's web. Colored beads and feathers are added to the outside of the hoop for symbolic meaning. The beads represent the spider. Some legends claim the spider eats the bad dreams. Others say the spider holds them in the web until Father Sun makes them disappear. Feathers attract good dreams and messages from the spirit world and direct them to the dreamer.

It is a custom to hang dream catchers in windows or above a bed as protection from bad dreams and negative energy. The small hole in the center allows only good energies and dreams to pass through to the sleeping dreamer.

The Ojibwa and Pawnee believed Spider Woman, an ancestral spirit, would go to each baby's cradleboard and spin a silken dream catcher above it. Is it possible that the spider at the Nativity performed this function, weaving a dream catcher web to protect the Holy Family from bad dreams and negative energy?

Many people practice the age-old tradition of cleaning house from floor to ceiling, getting rid of dust, clutter, and cobwebs in preparation for Christmas. It is a way to prepare our hearth and heart for the arrival of the Christ Child and the spirit of Christmas.

Legends tell of a poor family who followed this tradition. The young daughter had no fear of spiders. She felt sorry for them as they were swept, shoved, and shooed out of the house. She prayed that they would be allowed to enjoy Christmas with her family.

On Christmas Eve night, the sound of tiny footsteps awakened the little girl. The footfalls were so quiet that only a child could hear them. She rolled out of bed to investigate the noise and saw spiders marching into her home. She watched in horror as they climbed up the family's Christmas tree and wrapped it in their webs. The tree had no decorations because her family was too poor to afford them. Nevertheless, the tree's natural beauty was still better than the tangled webs the spiders had created.

The little girl crept back to bed in tears, regretting she had wished to include the spiders in her family's Christmas celebration.

During the night, the Christ Child visited the tree, as He does to all trees in homes on Christmas Eve, legend tells us. He changed the webs into glittering gold and silver strands of tinsel. The next morning, the family gathered to celebrate Christmas. Much to their surprise, their Christmas tree sparkled like diamonds.

Today, we decorate Christmas trees with strands of silver tinsel to represent the spider's web, the gift of the Christ Child. The best luck of all is to find a real spider web on your tree.

The Humpy-Back Camel

"I," said the camel, yellow and black,
"Over the desert, upon my back,
I brought Him a gift in the
Wise Men's pack."

—from "The Friendly Beast"

A MEDIEVAL FRENCH CAROL

Camels were the multipurpose, all-terrain land rovers of the ancient world. They were strong, reliable, and steadfast, which earned them the name Ship of the Desert. A camel can carry up to 1,000 pounds of cargo at speeds of almost 25 miles a day in extreme arid conditions.

The animal is also a source of meat, milk, and clothing for such desert cultures as the Bedouin. They call them *Ata Allah* (God's Gift). Camels are to desert dwellers what the buffalo were to Native Americans.

The camel can plod along for days in the blazing sun without taking a drink. It carries its water supply in its hump, people believed for centuries. Today, we know different.

A camel stores fat in its hump—a single hump if the camel is a Dromedary, a double hump if the camel is a Bactrian. A camel can lose up to 40 percent of its body mass when food and water are scarce. The fat in the hump helps keep the animal going. It lets the camel rehydrate at a rate of 25 gallons of water in 10 minutes.

The camel's hump has been a matter of speculation and imagination throughout history. Rudyard Kipling described how the camel got its much-discussed hump in one of his *Just So Stories*. In the beginning of the world, the camel's body was sleek like the horse and zebra. But, it was a lazy and aloof animal and refused to socialize or work with the other animals.

When asked to join in or help out, the camel responded with an insolent "humph." Its arrogant tone irritated the other animals. To silence its obnoxious reply, a desert magician known as the Djinn turned the camel's voiced "humph" into a physical hump and attached it to the camel's back.

Camels are at home in arid and semiarid environments. To cope with extreme heat and dehydration, they have physiological characteristics that give them an exotic and even comical appearance.

In addition to its distinctive hump, the camel is a composite of several special features. A double set of beautiful, long eyelashes protects its large, brown eyes from stinging sand kicked up by the wind. Its wide nostrils become slits during storms and prevent the camel from inhaling sand.

A biological thermostat allows the camel to conserve water by regulating its body temperature. Wide feet spread out for balance and help the camel avoid stumbling over rocks or sinking into sand. Its hooves are also insensitive to the stings and bites of desert insects and reptiles.

This amazing pack animal can be both charming and irritating. Its haughty expression borders on a smirk. Perhaps it's a warning. A camel can be quite rude. If annoyed, it shows its displeasure by spitting on its antagonist.

How the camel acquired its unmatched survival skills is an intriguing question. Perhaps the answer lies in a legend tied to the story of the Magi. It was on camels that the Magi rode following the Star of Bethlehem. Commonly referred to as the Three Wise Men, the Magi were possibly Zoroastrian priests. Their professions are not stated in the Bible, but we do know they were well educated in astronomy and astrology.

The Magi realized the new star in the east was a extraordinary sign. In the ancient world, celestial signs were believed to predict life-changing events. A star as bright as the Nativity star could even mean the crowning of a new ruler. The Magi decided to follow the star to learn what it meant.

Nativity reenactments often place three Magi and their camels at the stable with shepherds and sheep and other animals. The Magi were the last to arrive, stories tell us. However, the Bible does not give the number of Magi who visited. Three is suggested because of the number of gifts presented to the Christ Child.

Three is also a symbolic number that appears throughout the Bible. The Bible also states the Magi did not come on the night of Christ's birth, but later, possibly when the Holy Family was staying at a house in Bethlehem.

The Magi were wealthy because their choice of transportation was the camel. It was a status symbol of the ancient world. Only the rich and famous owned camels. The Magi also carried expensive gifts worthy only for a king: gold, which symbolized eternity; frankincense, used to consecrate temples and believed to banish evil and inspire awe; and myrrh, an expensive spice used as a cure-all and for burials of gods.

The Magi were eager to find out where the Wondrous Star was leading them. In their haste, they did not pack enough water for themselves or their camels. They pushed their animals onward without food, water, or rest. The camels responded to the Magi's urging. They raced across the desert thirsty and tired but without complaint or hesitation.

When they reached the Christ Child, the Magi and camels fell to their knees and worshiped Him. They thanked God for their safe and quick journey. In return, the Christ Child praised the camels for their courage to make such an exhausting trip. He blessed them with a wonderful gift—the ability to travel with ease over great distances without food, water, or rest.

Man's Best Animal Friend

When the Man waked up, he said,
"What is the Wild Dog doing here?"
And the Woman said, "His name is not
Wild Dog any more, but the First Friend,
because he will be our friend for
always and always and always."

The Cat that Walked by Himself—Rudyard Kipling

Dogs have been loyal companions to people for most of human history. Much like God's love, they are faithful, strong, and always present. Some dog fanciers claim God loved the dog so much, He gave it His name, but spelled it backwards.

The dog's history is ancient. Scientists have traced its ancestry to a small weasel-like animal called *Miacis*. They believe all dogs, wolves, and foxes descended from this common ancestor. It lived approximately 60 million years ago in northern Asia.

Dogs and humans share a paw-in-hand relationship. They have similar social traits: the dog lives in a pack; the human lives in a family. Both enjoy close friendly relationships and attention.

Cavemen in the Paleolithic Age domesticated dogs to help them hunt for game. The possibility of a morsel of food may have attracted the first dog to early man's campsite. Maybe their relationship developed into a work-for-food arrangement. Both benefited. The dog received food, warmth, and companionship; the man gained a helper to hunt, herd, and guard.

The dog was also associated with death and the afterlife. Ancient Egyptians worshiped the dog as a messenger from the dead. In Greek mythology, Cerberus, a three-headed dog, guarded Hades. Half a world away, the Maya of Mexico also believed the dog was a messenger of death. Many cultures believed dogs could see spirits and could anticipate death, especially the death of their master. Abraham Lincoln's dog howled and ran frantically through the White House shortly before Lincoln's assassination, one story relates.

Superstitions about dogs abound in many cultures, especially ones about a howling dog. For some Egyptians, Hebrews, Greeks, and Irish, a howling dog is a bad omen. Its mournful cry predicts death. In ancient Rome, the bawling of dogs was heard before Julius Caesar's death.

Perhaps its cousin, the wolf with its doleful wail made people beware of the dog. Stories of Little Red Riding Hood and the Three Little Pigs exaggerated the evil of the wolf and the fear it instilled in the people.

The dog is a prominent figure in Greek mythology. Orion, the Great Hunter, travels through the nighttime skies with his two hunting dogs, Canis Major and Canis Minor. Canis Major earned its position in the heavens by winning a race with a fox. Canis became the fastest animal in the world. Zeus rewarded the dog by placing it in the sky with Orion.

The star Sirius, known as the Dog Star, is a diamond in Canis Major's collar. Sirius means *scorching* or *sparkling* because it is closest to the sun from July 3 to August 11, a period of sweltering temperatures called the Dog Days of Summer.

Canis Minor, Orion's smaller dog, follows at the heels of Canis Major. Canis Minor was the favorite of Helen of Troy. Mythology says she placed it in the heavens to grant it immortality, so she could see it forever.

Life for the dog improved as human society became more developed and advanced. The dog's role in the family and community expanded from a working animal to a beloved family pet.

Many stories recount the loyalty and companionship of dogs. Excavators found the remains of a dog lying across a child in the ruins of Pompeii, the Roman city destroyed by Mount Vesuvius in 79 A.D. They speculate the dog was trying to protect the child.

In the Greek epic *Odyssey*, when Odysseus returned disguised as a beggar, his faithful dog, Argus, was the only creature to recognize him. After it greeted its master, Argus died.

The dog had kept a 20-year vigil waiting for its wandering master to return. Such stories acknowledge that the dog deserves the title Man's Best Friend.

But has that beloved title been accepted by all humankind? Perhaps not. Why wasn't Man's Best Friend at the Nativity event?

The Bible describes the dog in very unflattering terms. In Old Testament times, the dog was considered a scavenger, therefore, an unclean animal. It was banned by priests and could not be used in rituals or for sacrifices. To be called a *dog* was the worst insult. The modern jest or insult *dirty dog* is mild compared to biblical curses. Biblical scorn for the dog perhaps excluded the animal from the Nativity.

Only an old, seldom-quoted saying connects the

dog to the blessed stable. *A dog in a manger* describes a person who cannot use something and prevents other people from using it too. Because the manger had to be shared on the Nativity night, the dog had to stay away so the Christ Child could use it.

But what about the shepherds? They used dogs to herd their sheep. Isn't it possible that at least one dog would have come along with them to the manger? Once at the stable, a dog could have guarded against predators. In Native American Nativities, a wolf stands guard near the Christ Child.

Could it be that a wolf's lonesome howl at the moon is really a prayer of thanksgiving? If so, perhaps it's an eternal reminder to all canines that they weren't overlooked that blessed night. They, too, were a vital part of the menagerie at the manger.

EPILOGUE

For every beast of the forest is mine,
and the cattle upon a thousand hills.
I know all the fowls of the mountains:
and the wild beasts of the field are mine.

—Psalms 50:10-11

Folklore depicts the first Christmas as an enchanted time. Stars fell from the heavens to become beautiful blossoms that filled and surrounded the manger. Ordinary weeds became beautiful flowers. The once simple stable was transformed into a celebration of nature.

Many animals gathered at the manger to celebrate the birth of the Christ Child. On the Nativity's silent, holy night, as the menagerie at the manger surrounded the Newborn, each animal expressed its concern and joy to the world in its own manner and voice. The lullabies of the animals became the first Christmas carols to honor the King of Kings.

These customs continue today, so legends say. Each Christmas, veiled by midnight, animals in fields and pastures kneel and pay homage to the Christ Child. At that time, for one hour and one hour only, the animals are granted the sublime gift of speech.

The presence of the menagerie at the manger demonstrated God's love for all nature, not just for humankind. The animals' gift to us is a refreshing perspective of the world's most glorious birth.

As long as there are storytellers, the mystery and magic of the Nativity animals will captivate our minds and touch our souls. And, as each animal's story is retold, it will intrigue a new generation with the centuries-old question: This is just a legend—*isn't it?*

BIBLIOGRAPHY

Adams, Richard. *The Unbroken Web Stories and Fables.* New York: Crown Publishers, 1980.

Alderton, David. *Dogs*. New York: DK Publishing, Inc., 1993.

"Amerindian Christmas." *Aboriginal and Tribal New Nation News*. 2 January 2004. http://www.newnation.org/NNN-news-aboriginal.html.

Animals of the Nativity. Executive Producer, Amy Hillard. Animal Planet, December, 2003.

"A Spider's Web." By John H.Lienhard. *Engines of Our Ingenuity*. Episode 1069. Public Radio. Produced for KUHF-FM, Houston. Transcript.

Brown, Margaret Wise. *Christmas in the Barn*. New York: Harper & Row, 1952.

Byrd, Robert. *St. Francis and the Christmas Donkey*. New York: Dutton Children's Books, 2000.

Christmas Ornament Legends, Volumes I and II. Merck Family Old World Christmas, 2000.

Climo, Shirley. *Cobweb Christmas: The Tradition of Tinsel*. New York: Harper Collins, 2001.

Cole, Jacci. *Animal Communication: Opposing Viewpoints*. San Diego: Greenhaven Press, Inc., 1989.

"Concerning Dogs." *Internet Sacred Texts.com*. 14 March 2005. http://www.sacred-texts.com/neu/celt/ali/ali08l.htm.

Cunningham, Julia. *The Stable Rat and Other Christmas Poems*. New York: Greenwillow Books, 2001.

"Dog Stars of the Heavens." *K-9 Clickers Dog Training Services*. 13 March 2005. http://www.homepage.ntlworld.com/k.westgate/history4htm.

Ehret, Walter and Evans, George K. *The International Book of Christmas Carols*. New York: Prentice Hall, Inc. 1963.

Farber, Norma. *When It Snowed That Night.* New York: Harper Collins, 1993.

Feister, John Bookser. "St. Francis Preaches to the Birds." *American Catholic.org*. 2 September 2003. http://www.americancatholic.org/Features/Francisstories.asp.

"Goats and Spider Webs." By John H. Lienhard. *Engines of Our Ingenuity*. Episode 1717. Public Radio. Produced for KUHF–FM, Houston. Transcript.

"History of Dogs." *Dog Quotes.com*. Australia Media Pty Ltd. 3 March 2005. http://www.dogquotes.com.

Kipling, Rudyard. *Just So Stories*. New York: Henry Holt and Company, 1987.

Mackin, O.F.M., "Blessing of Animals." *American Catholic.org*. 2 September 2003. http://www.americancatholic.org/Features/Francis/blessings.asp.

Mitchell, P.J. "Dreamcatcher Legends." *Spiritual Network.net*. 27 July 2003. http://www.spiritualnetwork.net/ dreamcatcher/legends.htm.

Sheldrake, Rupert. *Dogs That Know When Their Owners Are Coming Home*. New York: Crown Publishers, 1999.

"Spider Facts." *Meadow Treasures 2003*. 27 July 2003. http://www.meadowtreasures.com/spiderfacts.htm.

"Taurus the Bull, The Legend and Myth." *Constellation Chamber*. 27 July 2003. http://www.novareinna.com/constellation/tauruslegend.html.

"The Cat in the Manger." *St. Florian on the Web*. 5 January 2005. http://www.florian.hegewisch.net/school/advent/xmascat.html.

The Holy Bible: King James Version. United States: World Publishing Co. 1954.

"The Legend of the Christmas Bell." *Rfamily4Him.* Homepage 2000-2003. 25 May 2004. http://www.geocities.com/Rfamily4Him/ChristmasBell.html.

Tucker, Suzetta. "ChristStory Christmas Legends." *ChristStory Christian Beastiary*. 1996. 27 May 2005. http://ww2.netnitco.net/users/legend01/xlegend.htm.

Ward, Helen. *The Animal's Christmas Carol*. Brookfield, CT: The Millbrook Press, 2001.

The Editorial Annex
Oklahoma City/Edmond, Oklahoma

The Editorial Annex is a communication consultancy and publishing house founded in Washington, D.C., 1991.

Editor & Publisher: Richard M. Crum
www.theeditorialannex.com

Design: Felton Stroud
Stroud Design, Inc., Oklahoma City, OK
www.strouddesign.com

Author's Website
www.for-evergreen.com

Illustrator's Website
www.scottallenstudio.com

Typeset in 12 point New Times Roman with 16 point leading.
Title and accent text in Celestia Antiqua.

Printing and binding through InterPress, Limited,
Four-color process inks on128 gsm matte text. Dust Jacket printed four-color process inks on 157 gsm gloss text with metallic foil stamp and lamination. Smythe sewn case binding, cloth with metallic foil stamp.